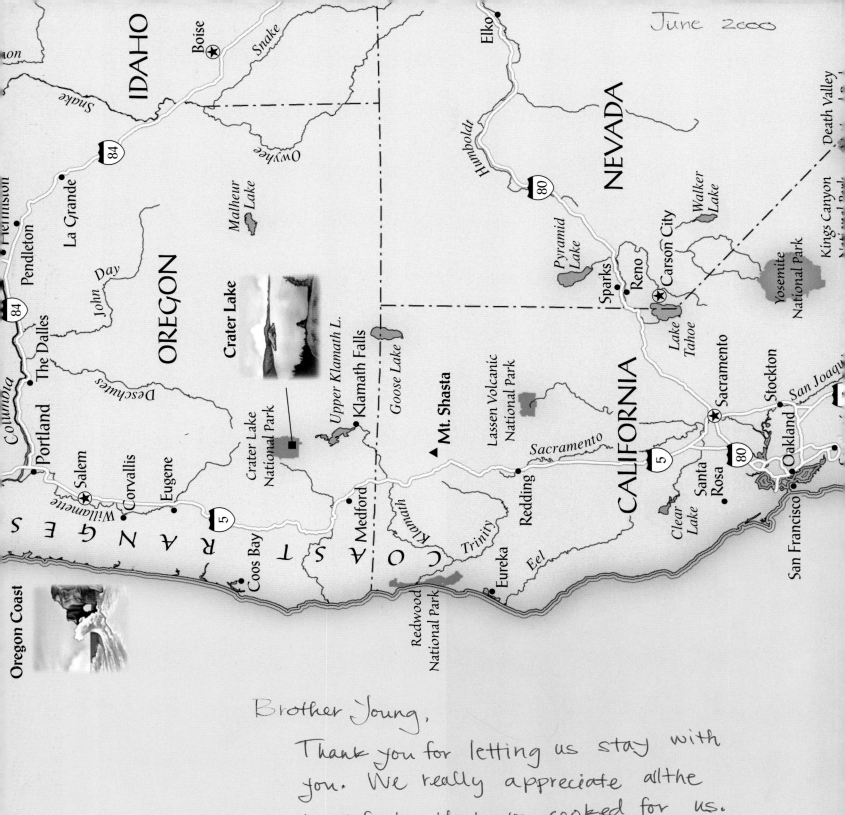

June 2000

IDAHO

Boise

Snake

Snake

NEVADA

Elko

Humboldt

84

Hermiston

Pendleton

La Grande

84

Malheur Lake

Owyhee

80

Pyramid Lake

Walker Lake

Death Valley

Kings Canyon National Park

OREGON

John Day

Deschutes

Crater Lake

Upper Klamath L.

Klamath Falls

Goose Lake

▲ Mt. Shasta

Lassen Volcanic National Park

Sparks

Reno

Carson City

Lake Tahoe

Yosemite National Park

Portland

Salem

Corvallis

Eugene

Willamette

Columbia

The Dalles

Crater Lake National Park

5

Medford

Klamath

Trinity

Redding

Sacramento

CALIFORNIA

Sacramento

Stockton

San Joaqu

5

Santa Rosa

Clear Lake

80

Oakland

S R A N G E S

C O A S T

Coos Bay

Eureka

Eel

Redwood National Park

San Francisco

Oregon Coast

Brother Young,

Thank you for letting us stay with
you. We really appreciate all the
breakfasts that you cooked for us.
The fresh fruit was GREAT!!
Thanks for your HUGS & KISSES!!
We hope you will enjoy this book.

♡

Kerry

Kaaryn

ANDREI SAVELIEV

CRESCENT BOOKS

NEW YORK

FRONT COVER: Sapphire-blue Crater Lake, Oregon's only national park, was formed almost eight thousand years ago when a volcano exploded. Heavy snows close the park much of the year. BACK COVER: Totems, or symbols of Native American clans carved onto poles and often painted, depict animals and other natural objects. These specimens stand in Vancouver's Stanley Park. PAGE 1: Michael Booth and a group of schoolchildren dedicated their Wagons Ho! statue outside the Umatilla County Museum in Pendleton, Oregon, to pioneers who moved westward on the Oregon Trail. PAGES 2–3: The 520-foot Space Needle, a landmark of the 1962 World's Fair in Seattle Center, is visible from just about everywhere in town and offers a splendid view of the city and Puget Sound.

This 1999 edition is published by Crescent Books®,
an imprint of
Random House Value Publishing, Inc.,
201 East 50th Street, New York, N.Y. 10022.

Crescent Books and colophon
are registered trademarks of
Random House Value Publishing, Inc.

Random House
New York • Toronto • London • Sydney • Auckland
http://www.randomhouse.com/

Printed and bound in China

Library of Congress Cataloging-in-Publication Data
Highsmith, Carol M., 1946–
Pacific Northwest /
Carol M. Highsmith and Ted Landphair.
p. cm. — (A photographic tour)
Includes index.
ISBN 0-517-20401-0 (hc: alk. paper)
1. Northwest, Pacific—Tours.
2. Northwest, Pacific—Pictorial works.
I. Landphair, Ted, 1942– . II. Title. III. Series:
Highsmith, Carol M., 1946–   Photographic tour.
F852.3.H54 1999   98–35691
917.9504´43—dc21   CIP

8 7 6 5 4 3 2 1

Project Editor: Donna Lee Lurker
Production Supervisor: Milton Wackerow
Designed by Robert L. Wiser, Archetype Press, Inc.,
Washington, D.C.

All photographs by Carol M. Highsmith unless otherwise credited: map by XNR Productions, page 5; painting by Albert Bierstadt, Portland Art Museum, gift of Henry F. Cabell, page 6; Friends of Timberline, pages 8, 10; Tillamook Creamery, Tillamook, Oregon, page 9; Columbia River Exhibition of History, Science and Technology Museum, pages 11, 17; U.S. Geological Survey, David A. Johnston Cascades Volcano Observatory, Vancouver, Washington, page 12; Red Shed Farm Museum, Deer Park, Washington, pages 13, 14–15, 16; Klondike Gold Rush National Historic Park, Seattle Unit, page 18; Seattle Times, page 19; Seattle Underground Tour, page 20; Laurel Point Inn, Victoria, British Columbia, page 21.

THE AUTHORS WISH TO THANK THE FOLLOWING FOR THEIR GENEROUS ASSISTANCE AND HOSPITALITY IN CONNECTION WITH THE COMPLETION OF THIS BOOK

B. C. Ferries, Vancouver-Victoria ferry

Best Western Inn, Gig Harbor, Washington

Best Western Inn, Prosser, Washington

Bethel Heights Farm Bed & Breakfast, Salem, Oregon

Carter House Country Inn, Eureka, California

Clipper Navigation, Victoria-Seattle ferry

Doubletree Hotel, Richland, Washington

Doubletree Hotel Lloyd Center, Portland

Green Cape Cod B&B, Tacoma

Howard Johnson Inn, La Grande, Oregon

Laurel Point Inn, Victoria, British Columbia

Listel Vancouver Hotel

Hotel Lusso, Spokane

O'Brien Mountain Inn, O'Brien, California

The Rose River Inn Bed & Breakfast, Astoria, Oregon

Tyee Hotel, Tumwater, Washington

Rochelle Adams, Seattle-King County News Bureau

Heather Day, Tourism Victoria

Janet Dotson, La Grande and Union County Visitors Bureau

Irene Hoadley, Salem, Oregon, Convention & Visitors Association

Kathleen Gordon-Burke, Eureka-Humboldt County Convention & Visitors Bureau, Eureka, California

Julie Gangler, Tacoma-Pierce County Visitor & Convention Bureau

Barbara Glover, Yakima Valley, Washington, Visitors & Convention Bureau

Linda Miller, Spokane Area Convention & Visitors Bureau

Dare Rasmussen, Sequim, Washington

Mica Ryan, Tourism British Columbia

Sally Sederstrom, Oregon Tourism Commission

Laura Serena, Tourism Vancouver

Bonnie Sharp, Redding Convention & Visitors Bureau, Redding, California

Deborah Wakefield, Portland Visitors Association

Tori Wilder Benson, Portland Visitors Association

Carrie Wilkinson-Tuma and Kelly Jones, Washington State Tourism

Pacific Northwest

California
Capital: Sacramento
Statehood: September 9, 1850 (31st state)
Area: 155,973 square miles (403,970 sq km)
Nickname: Golden State
State bird: California Valley Quail
State flower: Golden poppy
State tree: California redwood
State motto: *Eureka* ("I have found it")
Average January temperature: Sacramento, 45°F (7°C)
Average July temperature: Sacramento, 75°F (24°C)

Oregon
Capital: Salem
Statehood: February 14, 1859 (33d state)
Area: 96,003 square miles (248,647 sq km)
Nickname: Beaver State
State bird: Western meadowlark
State animal: Beaver
State flower: Oregon grape
State tree: Douglas fir
State motto: *Alis volat Propriis* ("She flies with her own wings")
Average January temperature: Portland, 40°F (4°C)
Average July temperature: Portland, 68°F (20°C)

Washington
Capital: Olympia
Statehood: November 11, 1889 (42d state)
Area: 66, 582 sq m (172,447 sq km)
Nicknames: Evergreen State, Chinook State
State bird: Willow goldfinch
State flower: Coast rhododendron
State tree: Western hemlock
State motto: *Al-Ki* (Native American word meaning "by and by")
Average January temperature: Seattle, 41°F (5°C)
Average July temperature: Seattle, 66°F (19°C)

British Columbia
Capital: Victoria
Joined Canadian Confederation: July 20, 1871
Area: 365,948 square miles (951,465 sq km)
Motto: *Splendor Sine Occasu* ("Splendor without waning")
Average January temperature: Victoria, 38°F (3°C)
Average July temperature: Victoria, 61°F (16°C)

PACIFIC OCEAN

N

0 50 100 150 200
Distance in miles

QUEEN CHARLOTTE ISLANDS

Prince Rupert
Skeena
Banks Island
Hecate Strait

Stuart Lake
Nechako Reservoir
Prince George
Fraser

COAST MOUNTAINS

ROCKY MOUNTAINS

ALBERTA

West Road
Quesnel Lake

BRITISH COLUMBIA

Williams Lake

Jasper National Park

Kinbasket Lake

Banff National Park

Glacier National Park

Fraser

Kamloops

Shuswap Lake

Upper Arrow Lake

Columbia

Queen Charlotte Strait

Powell River

Lillooet

Okanagan Lake Kelowna

Lower Arrow Lake

Kootenay Lake

VANCOUVER ISLAND

Port Alberni
Nanaimo
Vancouver

Victoria Parliament Building

Victoria
Strait of Juan de Fuca

North Cascades National Park

Columbia

Lake Pend Oreille

Space Needle

Olympic National Park

Seattle

Olympia

WASHINGTON

Spokane Coeur d'Alene

Mt. Rainier National Park

90

Clearwater

Mount St. Helens

Longview

Astoria

Walla Walla

82

Salmon

Columbia

Hermiston

Oregon Coast

Portland The Dalles

Pendleton

84

COAST RANGES

Salem

Willamette

Corvallis

Eugene

Deschutes

John Day

La Grande

84

IDAHO

Boise

Crater Lake

Crater Lake National Park

Malheur Lake

Upper Klamath L.

Owyhee

Snake

Medford

Klamath Falls

Goose Lake

Redwood National Park

Klamath

Mt. Shasta

Humboldt

Elko

Trinity

Lassen Volcanic National Park

Eureka

Eel

Redding

Sacramento

Pyramid Lake

80

CALIFORNIA

Sparks

Reno

Carson City

NEVADA

Clear Lake

Santa Rosa

Lake Tahoe

Walker Lake

Sacramento

80

Stockton

Yosemite National Park

San Francisco Oakland

San Joaquin

5

Kings Canyon National Park

Death Valley National Park

San José

THE FIRST IMAGE ONE CONJURES UP ABOUT THE PACIFIC Northwest is its expanse of forests. Washington is the Evergreen State, and there is a stand of Douglas firs next to a prairie schooner on the Oregon state flag. Far-northern California's sequoias and other redwoods—many soaring three hundred feet or more—can blot out the sun. And part of British Columbia's "splendor without waning" is its stunning breadth of forests. But after a visit to the region, it is the intriguing smells that one remembers. It is the *scent* of evergreen needles, fresh-cut timber, and the tangy smell of Pacific Northwest conifers that amazes, braces, and lingers.

Deep in the region's woods, especially amidst the lowland fog in the Cascade and Coastal ranges and the rain forest in Washington's Olympic Peninsula, the smell of newfallen rain refreshes, too. West of the coastal mountains the region can be drizzly, and the Olympic Peninsula, in particular, is lapped by the warm, moist ocean air that rides above the Pacific's Japanese current; the Peninsula endures an average 150 inches of rain a year. But the average annual rainfall in Seattle and Portland—both well inland—is half that of Little Rock's, barely 60 percent of the rainfall that pelts New Orleans or Mobile, and thirteen times *less* than the rain totals on Mount Waialeale on the Hawaiian island of Kauai—the rainiest spot on earth. Except in wintertime, the Pacific Northwest cities are rarely damp and gloomy for long.

The smells of the sea remain in one's memory too, for the people of the Pacific Northwest take to sailboats, ferries, cruise ships, and fishing boats as readily as they travel by car. Beaches are plentiful but often far too rocky, and the water too cold, for swimming. The faint odors here are of kelp and fresh driftwood, whole sodden tree trunks washed downstream from logging camps, tiny mollusks uncovered at low tide, and crackling beach fires. There is the smell of halibut, tuna, and Dungeness crabs hauled ashore in giant trawlers and tiny fishing boats as well as that of salmon smoking on grills along the piers and in commercial smokehouses in every good-sized coastal town.

There is a bouquet in the air, too, around the thousands of acres of apple, cherry, and loganberry orchards and strawberry fields. Oregon and Washington are leading producers of zesty peppermint and of flowers grown for bulbs and seeds. The forests, canyons, and mountain meadows abound with wildflowers—lupines, fragrant lavender, Indian paintbrush, phlox, pink rhododendrons, and aromatic wild roses—and the Pacific Northwest boasts cultivated perennial gardens on the scale of southern England's. The Butchart Gardens, established in 1904 in an old limestone quarry on British Columbia's Vancouver Island, for instance, features such splendors as cactus-flowered dahlias, Tibetan blue poppies, Dutch tulips, and other blooms from anemones to zinnias. So many varieties that Butchart Gardens maintains a "plant identification centre" to help visitors identify them all.

Who could forget the smell of exotic coffees? It wafts from thousands of coffeehouses, espresso bars, specialty coffee kiosks in malls, carts on the street, espresso booths inside grocery stores, ethnic restaurants, and even gas stations. Throughout the region—even in the tiniest interior towns—there are drive-through coffee stands. In all of these places, one can choose from among rich and sometimes flavored coffees, thick espresso, latté (strong coffee with steamed milk and the froth produced during steaming), cappucino (espresso with more froth and less milk), café au lait (borrowed from French Louisiana), and still more varieties. In the Pacific Northwest, coffee isn't coffee unless it is preceded by at least three adjectives, as in a "grande double mocha skinny (made with skim milk) latté." America's coffee craze started in

Albert Bierstadt, one of America's greatest landscape artists, painted this view of Oregon's Mount Hood in oil on canvas in 1869. Trained in Germany, Bierstadt traveled to the far western United States in search of scenery to rival that of the German and Swiss Alps. This painting hangs in the Portland Art Museum.

ALL INDIANS CENTENNIAL ASTORIA ORE

Representatives of several Native American tribes gathered at Astoria, Oregon, America's first western settlement, which was established at the mouth of the mighty Columbia River in 1811 by the Pacific Fur Trading Company.

Seattle in the mid-1980s and spread south and east; today the American Coffee Association estimates there are ten thousand or more specialty coffee shops across the country. Sipping in Seattle is still in fashion, and it is not unusual to find a Starbuck's, Seattle's Best Coffee, and one or two generic coffee spots within a few doors of each other. Residents tell you it is a by-product of the area's high-tech sophistication and "laid-back lifestyle." Washington's official motto—taken from the Chinook dialect—after all, is *Alki*, meaning "by and by."

Tea houses are springing up in the region, too. Perhaps it is not the product but the brewing process that so fascinates people for the region is the epicenter of a microbrewery explosion as well. Portland alone has more than forty microbreweries and one hundred brewpubs. "Craft" brewers can be found throughout the rest of Washington, British Columbia, and Northern California as well. The eruption in the number of small, often neighborhood, breweries coincided with the buyouts and consolidations of large, nationwide brewing companies marketing pasteurized, pale (aficionados say "watered down") lagers and "light" beers. Regional breweries like Pyramid in Seattle, BridgePort in Portland, Humboldt in Arcata, California, and Granville Island in Vancouver found a niche with stronger ales, porters, stouts, and pilsners—also often bottled but not usually pasteurized. Taste, not long shelf lives, was their forté. Microbreweries—producing fewer than twenty-five-thousand barrels a year—made little effort to widely distribute their brews, preferring to capture loyal, local followings with specialty beers. Even smaller brewpubs, turning out mere hundreds of barrels of suds a year behind the bar, popped up in big Pacific Northwest cities and little towns alike. Many adopted eccentric names: Engine House (No. 9) in Tacoma; Rock Bottom in Seattle; Scuttlebutt in Everett, Washington; Hair of the Dog in Portland; Mia and Pia's in Klamath Falls, Oregon; Red, White, and Brew in Red-

ding, California; and Knucklehead in Victoria, British Columbia. Just as Pacific Northwest coffee drinkers are fond of comparing the merits of various beans and blends, brewpub conversations turn to the proper techniques of a "good pour" or the proper size of a head. Somehow, despite the idle chatter at these brewpubs, coffeehouses, tea parlors, and Internet chat rooms, work gets done.

A surprising amount of it, considering the region's woodsy and marine images, is on farms and ranches east of the Cascades. There, the smells include those of new-mown wheat or alfalfa hay, mounds of freshly harvested potatoes, cattle clustered at feed lots, or sheep bunched together for shearing. The "rain shadow" cast by the coastal mountains leaves these flatlands relatively dry and warm, resulting in a long and frost-free crop season of 250 days or more each year.

The staggering beauty of the Pacific Northwest's imposing snow-clad peaks—Ranier, Hood, Baker, Shasta, and others, towering so close to lowland rain forests—has no special scent, of course, save for the bracing air of the great outdoors. It is here—and in the region's deep ravines, along its wild seashore, across the wooded San Juan Islands above Puget Sound, on thousands of freshwater lakes, and throughout the length of the wide Columbia and wild Snake and other rivers—that hunting, fishing, whitewater rafting, birding, and jouncy off-road driving are passions. The Snake, rated one of the nation's top three whitewater courses, cuts a canyon along the Oregon-Idaho border that is deeper than the Grand Canyon.

The Spaniards who first poked around the coast of the Pacific Northwest in the mid-1500s were not interested in sights or smells. They were looking for glory and gold. They claimed the lands but did not bother to establish settlements along the rocky shore. British explorers,

A fertile valley just inland from Oregon's coast has been likened to Wisconsin's dairy country. Thousands of visitors still peer into the windows of the Tillamook Creamery, the West Coast's largest cheesemaker.

searching for a Northwest Passage between the Atlantic and Pacific oceans, followed two centuries later. Russian trappers sailed nearby, too, eventually establishing a colony at Fort Ross in Northern California. When the sea otter supply played out a few years later, most Russians departed for home, leaving behind a few churches and other structures. Fur traders of many nationalities soon followed into the Pacific Northwest's interior. They included Robert Gray who crossed the bar of the Columbia River—which Gray named after his ship, the *Columbia Rediviva*—in 1792. The pathfinding expedition of Meriwether Lewis and William Clark followed that river to the sea thirteen years later. John Jacob Astor made a fortune from his Pacific Fur Company, established by his minions in Astoria, the Oregon Country's first permanent settlement at the mouth of the Columbia in 1811. A concerted incursion of other Americans, led by Methodist and Roman Catholic missionaries and "mountain men" from the Rockies, began in Oregon soon thereafter.

The trickle became a human tidal wave beginning in the 1840s with the arrival at the land office at Oregon City—now a suburb of Portland—of Midwest farm families who had trudged from Missouri along the "Oregon Trail" to what they hoped would be the "gates of Eden" in the fertile Willamette Valley. Estimates of the number of pioneers vary from three hundred thousand to five hundred thousand. Imbued with "Oregon fever," they came mostly on foot, leading their teams of mules, horses, or oxen that pulled all their worldly possessions in prairie schooner wagons. To their surprise, it was not the rugged Rocky Mountains that proved to be their greatest impediment, for a broad and gentle pass through the Rockies had been found in southern Wyoming. The most arduous climb was indeed at Eden's gate, over eastern Oregon's Blue Mountains, which offered no passes at all.

The "Great Outdoors" has long been an attraction of the Pacific Northwest. Here a family poses on an expedition to the foothills of Mount Hood—still a favorite hiking and ski destination near Portland.

Great Britain, whose subjects had engaged in their own westward migration across Canada, also coveted the rich Pacific Northwest, and, for a time, control of the nebulous "Oregon Country" was in dispute. Americans sought to push the British northward, all the way to latitude 54°40′N in the Yukon, and a rallying cry of supporters of James K. Polk in the U.S. presidential election of 1844 was "Fifty-four forty or fight!" Knowing that its claim to the Pacific Northwest rested largely in the hands of a few Hudson Bay fur company traders and the valiant Northwest Mounted Police, the British took what they could get in a treaty struck in 1846. It conceded all lands south of the forty-ninth parallel (save for the southern tip of Vancouver Island) to the United States but ended Americans' designs on Canadian territory.

Two years later, the Oregon Territory, including what is now all of Washington State and much of Idaho, was organized. Settlement of the western portion proceeded in two distinct clumps—one to the south of the Columbia around Portland at the confluence of the Willamette River, and the other along the western shore of Puget Sound. In 1853, the northern reaches broke off as their own territory, named "Washington" after the first U.S. president. Truncated Oregon became a state with its present boundaries in 1859. Washington lost some of its lands to a new Idaho Territory and waited until 1889 before becoming the nation's forty-second state. For much of this period the bulk of Northern California and far-western Canada were wilderness. The latter's mainland did not unite with Vancouver Island to form British Columbia until 1866. The arrival of transcontinental railroads there, in Washington and Oregon, and in Northern California over the next two decades spurred rampant development of the region.

In the years since, the Pacific Northwest's timber and agricultural riches as well as its

The swift Columbia River that separates much of Oregon and Washington is famous as a salmon spawning ground. It has also been the site of powerboat, and later hydroplane, races over the years.

When Washington's volcanic Mount Saint Helens erupted on May 18, 1980, it blew away twelve hundred feet of itself, obliterated or charred thousands of acres of forestland, and killed at least thirty-four people.

extensive mining, hydroelectric and nuclear energy production, aluminum smelting and refining, and, later, aerospace and computer industries, have expanded the region's economy. So have tourists drawn to the region's boundless natural wonders that include Mounts Ranier and Hood, and the remnants of Mount Saint Helens—which erupted in 1980 and around which barren hillsides and charred timber can still be seen. Today Mount Saint Helens is a fairly inaccessible 110,000-acre "national volcanic monument." The closest that visitors can get to the mountain today is the Johnston Ridge Observatory, five miles away, where the still-steaming lava dome, crater, and landslide deposit can be seen. Crater Lake, one of the world's most renowned lakes—owing to the deep blue hue of its waters—is in southern Oregon. It is set in the depression left from the explosions of the now-extinct Mount Mazama Volcano.

A comprehensive tour of the Pacific Northwest might begin in extreme Northern California. This is a land far different from the rest of California. It is a trove of national forests, wild rivers, precipitous mountain roads, and craggy coastline more akin to green Oregon, Washington, and western Canada. The far-northern California counties are a dense, woodsy place where not just ice and deer pose road hazards, so do hard Gray Pine cones, which fall like rocks and do damage to vehicles and noggins. From here, reservoirs, dams, and aqueducts divert water to the state's arid Central Valley and to Southern California. Here, too, miners at the turn of the twentieth century washed away whole mountains with hoses called "hydraulic monitors" in their search for gold.

The heart of the region is the Sacramento River, a lush corridor that knifes past 14,162-foot Mount Shasta—a dormant volcano—to its north, Mount Lassen to the east, and the "Trinity Alps," glistening in the west. The river courses into Redding, an old railroad supply center for mines in Northern California and central Oregon that calls itself "Another California." Here, and in surrounding towns like Shasta, Yreka, and Alturas, are state historic parks, railroad and Native American museums, artesian hot springs, numerous waterfalls, and elegant Victorian homes. In Red Bluff, along the Sacramento, is a house that once belonged to William Ide, the only president of California. In 1846, Ide, a Colusi County judge, was chosen president of the "Bear Flag Republic," which lasted barely a month. Among the other attractions in California's "Shasta Cascade" area: fly fishing, snowmobiling, houseboating on Shasta Lake, trail riding, and jet skiing.

To the west, closer to the coast, looms the majestic Redwood Forest, home to the world's tallest—and some of its oldest—trees. The Redwood Highway, or "Avenue of the Giants," through Humboldt Redwoods State Park leads visitors past such wonders as a drive-through living tree, a twenty-foot-wide room carved from a single tree, and the "Immortal Tree," thought to be 950 or more years old. Indeed, the giant redwoods—*Sequoia Semperviren,* or "sequoia ever-living"—are one of the oldest known life forms on earth. They grow only here, in the humid coastal climate of Northern California and southern Oregon.

With more artists per capita than any other California county, Humboldt County is California's art capital. A good place to find one is in Eureka, a city of multiple murals, where artists also display their work in "phantom galleries." These are empty storefronts that have been turned into galleries as part of Eureka's budding cultural arts district. South of Eureka and across the "Fernbridge," thought to be the world's oldest reinforced concrete bridge, is the intricately restored Victorian village of Ferndale, a historic immigrant melting pot and dairy village. Here, the Portuguese Holy Ghost Celebration and the Scandinavian Mid-Summer Festival are still annual events.

The rocky coast of Oregon—which, by the way, natives pronounce "ORR-ih-gun," not "ORR-ih-gone"—is accessed from U.S. Highway 101, which roughly parallels it and sometimes dips right down to the sea. From the north, the coastline begins in Astoria, the oldest American settlement west of the Rocky Mountains. Here, atop Coxcomb Hill, visitors can climb the 123-foot Astoria Column—inscribed in 1926 with scenes from Lewis and Clark's arrival at the Pacific Ocean and other events—for unsurpassed views of the mouth of the Columbia River, the Washington shore, and the coastal mountain range. Other Oregon shore sites heading southward: Seaside, Oregon's first seashore resort, where a statue marks the end of the Lewis and Clark Trail; Tillamook, supply center for Oregon's thriving dairy industry where one finds the largest cheese factory on the West Coast; a blimp hangar, now a Naval Air Station museum, where lighter-than-airships patrolled the coastline looking for submarines during World War II; Lincoln City, whose beach is often rated the best place in North America to fly a kite; Depoe Bay, reputed to be the world's smallest harbor; Newport, home of a hands-on marine science center; Seal Rock, famous for its wooden "chainsaw sculptures"; a forty-mile swath of incredible dunes—some hundreds of feet high—from Florence to North Bend; bustling Coos Bay, largest city on the Oregon Coast; and Port Orford, the most westerly incorporated city in the contiguous United States. The main attraction, of course, is the coastline itself with its treacherous black rocks that jut menacingly from the surf. Three merry family occasions along the shore take place in May (Bandon), June (Cannon Beach), and August (Lincoln City) respectively. These are sandcastle festivals, a beach lover's delight.

A beefy John Deere representative drew a crowd in eastern Washington in 1910 by showing that even a young man could pull his company's latest plow through the sod. Imagine what horses could do!

Frank Salzgeber shows off his threshing rig while J. M. Davis shows off his heading outfit on Davis's ranch outside Coulee City, Washington, in 1918. Horses still provided most of the horsepower on the prairie.

Portland, Oregon's largest city and one of the nation's leading exportation centers, is a remarkably self-contained city by design. Under Mayor Tom McCall in the late 1970s, and with the cooperation of county and suburban officials, it drew a simple line around the metropolitan area. This boundary has expanded outward, but its rigid purpose is still in place. Inside the line, carefully controlled urban growth is permitted. Outside—sometimes even on the other side of a city street—forests, farms, and open space must be maintained. Developers howled at the idea. They warned of a loss of jobs, but the opposite has occurred. Factories and high-tech campuses arose, and both the population and home prices soared—without unchecked sprawl. Still, downtown Portland is home to the nation's largest urban wilderness, the nearly five-thousand-acre Forest Park. The city even tore up a downtown freeway and replaced it with a delightful riverfront park whose many festivals have helped keep residents in town and the downtown alive at night. There is a dedicated transit mall, parts of which are closed to automobile traffic; "ART" the "cultural bus" that takes visitors on a tour of natural and cultural attractions; and several walkable shopping districts, including the city's own Nob Hill. Visits to downtown parks will reveal why Portland is known as the "Rose City." So will finding a place in the crowd at the nation's second-largest all-blossom parade, the Grand Floral Parade during the Portland Rose Festival each June. An alliterative writer at the city's visitors' association described Portland as a city of "books, beer, bikes, and blooms."

Portland is also the gateway to Mount Hood—home of rustic Timberline Lodge built by Works Progress Administration workers during the Great Depression—and the Columbia River Gorge, a sixty-mile stretch of basaltic cliffs that rise as high as three thousand feet above the wide river. Along the historic Columbia River Highway, Florentine viaducts, cut by Italian stonecutters, are cantilevered high into the cliffs, and frequent turn-offs afford delightful views of seventy-seven brilliant waterfalls. One, Multnomah Falls, the second-highest waterfall in the nation (behind Yosemite National Park's Lower Falls in California), is Oregon's most-visited tourist attraction.

Oregon even has its own Mardi Gras of sorts. It is the annual Graffiti Weekend each July in Roseburg, gateway to Crater Lake and the Oregon Caves National Monument. The name springs not from scrawlings on building walls but from the movie *American Graffiti*, the paean to the 1950s. For Roseburg's parade, six hundred or more classic cars—vintage 1960 or older—parade past more than twenty-five thousand spectators. In its first years, beginning in 1981, the

event had true Mardi Gras trappings including carousing, but in the years since organizers have steadily converted it into a strictly family affair. The same weekend in the nearby community of Winston, newer cars, motorcycles, and other motorized contraptions also drive in review.

Other southern Oregon attractions include the Oregon Shakespeare Festival in Ashland, which offers eleven plays in repertoire from mid-February through October; the Harry and David fruit-by-mail operation and country village in Medford; outfitters, recreational vehicle facilities, and campgrounds along the wild and scenic Rogue River at Grants Pass; three scenic byways and several covered bridges; and Oregon's largest natural lake near Klamath Falls.

In the high desert country of Central Oregon around towns like Bend and Antelope and Sisters, ranchers raise everything from cattle to llamas to reindeer. There are numerous golf resorts and dude ranches in the area, and in the wintertime, one can catch a ride behind sled dogs at Mount Bachelor. Parts of eastern Oregon are what the state's official travel guide calls "lonesome territory . . . a thirty-five-million-year work in progress." La Grande, an important stop on the Oregon Trail, is the hub of the rich Grande Ronde Valley with its great gulches. So breathtaking is the progression of peaks in the nearby Wallowa Mountains that they are known as the "Switzerland of America." Pendleton, in the heart of ranch country, hosts the Pendleton Round-Up, one of America's oldest and most famous rodeos. There are also smaller rodeos somewhere in eastern Oregon every weekend from early May through mid-September. In the town of John Day is the remarkable Kim Wah Chung & Co. Museum—an old trading post, Chinese labor exchange, and opium den that has been turned into a storyboard for the early history of Chinese laborers in the Pacific Northwest. Outside of town is the John Day Fossil Beds National Monument, which covers hundreds of square miles and includes geological formations and skeletal remains millions of years old. John Day was a trapper who was captured by Indians, stripped naked, and set free near The Dalles on the Columbia River. That is nowhere near Grant County, where the town that bears his name is located, and it is thought that he never set foot there. The John Day River reaches the area, however, and a town bearing his name sprang up anyway. Day is such a legendary figure in Oregon that three different places claim he is buried there!

The countryside across the state line in eastern Washington looks just as remote, and just as dusty as that of eastern Oregon until one reaches the irrigated fields around Washington's Tri-Cities of Pasco, Kennewick, and Richland. Walla Walla, not far away, was one of the first inland settlements in the Northwest. Its name comes from a Native American word for "many waters." Agriculture is central to life here, too. So important, in fact, that a local Chamber of Commerce representative listed the sweet onion as one of Walla Walla's tourist attractions.

Northward past a fertile hilly region called the Palouse lies Spokane, the largest city between Seattle and Minneapolis. This is a vibrant city whose downtown spreads from Riverfront Park along the Spokane River, whose picturesque falls provide power to the area. The city's most imposing landmark is the Great Northern Clock Tower. It was built by the Great Northern Railroad in 1902 as the signature feature of its big Spokane depot. Only the tower remains. Many of the grandiose old buildings that *do* remain in Spokane—including the Spokane Club, Davenport Hotel, the "Patsy" Clark Mansion (now a fine restaurant), and the Campbell House (today a city museum)—were designed for local mining and railroad barons during the turn-of-the-century Age of Elegance by local architect Kirtland Cutter.

"Country leisure" is the attraction of the Yakima Valley in the heart of Washington. Here, stretching over three hundred fifty thousand acres of patchwork pastures in an irrigated valley—the nation's fifth-largest producer of vegetables and fruits—is a cornucopia of small farms yielding asparagus, eggplant, apricots, winter pear, mint, Chukar cherries, all kinds of berries, pumpkins, and thirty other types of fruits and vegetables. Trellises in perfect rows hold up bright green hops destined for microbreweries throughout the Pacific Northwest. There is even an American Hop Museum in the town of Toppenish, which also invites visitors to "neckbend epic Western art murals over an espresso or wagon ride." Roadside stands offer everything from pastel blossoms to "ouch cacti." This is also Washington's wine country, which is home to more than thirty winemakers whose viticulturists delight in debating the merits of each harvest's yield.

Spokane had been rebuilt in this early twentieth-century photo following a devastating fire in 1898. A temporary bridge spanned the Spokane River above its famous falls. The stately Review *building, center, was unscathed in the fire.*

Seattle, an increasingly prominent and globally competitive city in the midst of a metropolitan region of more than 2.6 million people, is the region's most notable crossroads of peoples, cultures, technologies, and transportation. It is a place where Yakima apples go out and New Zealand kiwi fruit comes in, where tourists from across America head by air or sea to Alaska, western Canada, and the Far East, where more than four hundred international firms have a presence, and where the value of goods shipped through Seattle to Japan is nearly double that sent to nearby Canada. The Pacific Northwest fisheries industry, based in Seattle, supplies one-half the nation's seafood. A fisherman's terminal provides moorage for seven hundred fishing vessels as well as resupplying and repair facilities for giant trawlers. The city ranks third in the nation in the percentage of professional and technical employees among its workforce, and third in percentage of adults who have completed college. The Boeing aircraft company, the region's largest employer, is also America's largest exporter. Microsoft, the world's leading software manufacturer for personal computers, is headquartered in suburban Redmond.

Seattle, named the "Emerald City" for its many green hills, is home to Pike Place Market, the nation's oldest continuously operating farmers' market and, as one writer called it, "free-form funhouse." Fish fly through the air here, street performers provide music and comic relief, and vendors and craftspeople hawk their wares. Up the hill is *Hammering Man*, Jonathan Borofsky's post-modern sculpture outside the Seattle Art Museum. The city's colorful trolleys, imported from Australia, operate from Pier 70 to Pioneer Square and the International District, stopping at the Seattle Aquarium and elsewhere. Across town, the seventy-four-acre Seattle Center—at the base of the 605-foot-high Space Needle that was the trademark of the 1962 World's Fair—holds the city's science center, opera and ballet theaters, children's museum, and

In 1943 the Pentagon set up a top-secret plant to produce plutonium for warheads on the Hanford military reservation near Richland, Washington. Now closed, the plant was the site of frequent protests.

Seattle was a boomtown in 1898. Thousands of frenzied gold prospectors streamed through town on their way to Canada's Klondike region via southern Alaska. Seattle merchants prospered by outfitting and provisioning the miners.

basketball and hockey arena. Downtown is just a startling ninety *seconds* away by monorail. The harbor is a cacophony of seaplanes, houseboats, criss-crossing ferries, high-speed catamarans, sailboats, cruise ships, container vessels, and even kayaks. At the city's Ballard Locks, tourists love to gape at the sight of a lock full of oceangoing vessels being raised or lowered as much as twenty-six feet, depending on the tide, between Puget Sound and freshwater levels. The term "Skid Row"—originally Skid *Road*—was born in Seattle; it was a road used to skid timber down from the hills to Elliott Bay.

Seattle has become the takeoff point for cruises up Puget Sound and past Vancouver Island and spectacular Inside Passage fjords to Skagway, Alaska. Out of Anacortes, north of Seattle, tourists with plenty of time can begin the four-hundred-mile "Cascade Loop" driving tour eastward through the heart of the Cascade Mountains. Sights vary wildly from beautiful saltwater beaches and historic towns on Whidbey and Fidalgo islands in Puget Sound to the quiet Bavarian-style village of Leavenworth in the mountain foothills to forested bowls ringed by mountains in the Methow Valley. Most drivers take the Cascade Loop in a counterclockwise direction for a single reason: the magnificent east-to-west approach to Washington Pass, east of Mount Baker, far surpasses the view from west to east.

Heading west—instead of out of Anacortes by ferry—one reaches the San Juan Islands, 175 of which have been named. Their total number varies with the tide: up to 786 at low tide, fewer than 460 at high tide. Popular vacation destinations for decades, the San Juans are prized for their scenery and—even more important—their serenity. Cows and sheep graze in open pastures, hay is cut and baled, and yachts glide through deep channels cut by glaciers. The number of vacation homes is growing, but large developments are rare. The islands remain a day-tripper's paradise.

The Olympic Peninsula, Washington's "Green Kingdom" that sticks up the west side of Puget Sound like a thumb, seems like two separate time capsules: one, in the small, quiet towns, leads to the turn of the twentieth century; the other, in the region's Olympic Mountains and rain forest, to far earlier times. In little Port Angeles, one can grab a "footlong" at the Dogs-A-Foot hotdog stand beneath the nineteenth-century Lewis Building, which once housed a clothing emporium. Here, too, is the 1889 Captain H. L. Tibbals Building, home of the Palace Hotel. In its early days, the hotel was known as the "Palace of Sweets," and not because of any candy shop. It was the home and workplace of "ladies of the night." Here, a ghost reputedly beckons guests to Room 4 in particular, for reasons that are not entirely clear. Freight tunnels spider underneath Port Townsend.

Other natural attractions beckon visitors to the peninsula. Wild berries grow in abundance. Among them: huckleberries, black caps (a small black raspberry), and salmonberries (a sour, red or orange raspberry-looking fruit). More than ten thousand species of edible mushrooms have been catalogued in the peninsula's mist-shrouded meadows and woodlands. There are even "mushroom maps" of the region. Caution: hip-pocket guides to the area's mushrooms remind neophytes that there are also several species of these fungi that will kill you—and quickly!

Visitors are often surprised to find glaciers and good-sized mountain peaks on the Olympic Peninsula. The peninsula is so often shrouded in fog that a glimpse of the 7,965-foot Mount Olympus can be startling. This mountain receives more than two hundred inches of precipitation a year. Naturally, it begins as snow whose runoff has formed sixty named glaciers and the sizable Lake of the Gods inside Olympic National Park. This park is often described as three parks in one: the Olympic Coast, with the West Coast's longest stretch of wilderness shoreline; the Olympic Mountains, whose panorama is best viewed from overlooks along Hurricane Ridge; and a temperate rain forest replete with ferns and old-growth trees. The rain forest, which receives more than twelve *feet* of precipitation annually, is recognized internationally as a "Biosphere Reserve." Understandably, organized hiking is a favorite activity throughout the national park.

Farther down the Washington coast, a full-scale replica of the *Lady Washington*, a-square rigger that was the first American vessel to explore the Pacific Northwest Coast in 1788, sails from Aberdeen up the Chehalis River estuary where sightings of bald eagles, osprey, great blue herons—and an occasional whale—are common. The replica tall ship was launched in 1989 during Washington's centennial celebration.

Tacoma is the "jumping off point" for the Olympic Peninsula. Only the shortsighted would dismiss Tacoma as a forgettable step-sister to Seattle—an impression that is left by its second billing at Seattle-Tacoma ("Sea-Tac") International Airport. Genteel Tacoma—called the "City of Destiny" when, as a sawmill town, it was the western terminus of the first railroad to reach the Northwest—is home to the state history museum, one of seven U.S. manuscript library museums, two military museums, and a Native American museum. Inside Port Defiance Park is Fort Nisqually, a restored Hudson's Bay Company trading post as well as Camp Six, an open-air exhibit that tells the history of Washington's steam-powered logging

In this 1967 photo, Herbert Carroll smiles bravely as his two-ton street clock, which had stood for more than fifty years, was moved to his store's new address in downtown Seattle.

You can still see remnants of these 1878 storefronts from the original Pioneer Square during a tour of Underground Seattle. They are in fact all underground —literally buried by later downtown development.

operations. Today, Tacoma's deep-water port is the sixth-largest in North America. Below Tacoma is Olympia where Washingtonians modeled their 1928 capitol building after the U.S. Capitol in Washington, D.C.

Across the Peace Garden at the U.S.-Canadian border is Vancouver, Canada's third-largest city. It hosted a world exposition in 1986 that was expected to attract twelve million visitors. Instead, 21.3 million came, and Vancouver was "discovered" by the world. Today about one-fourth of its eight million or so annual overnight guests come from the United States. Routinely chosen as one of the world's top ten "best destinations" by *Condé Nast Traveler* magazine, it rates with Rio de Janeiro and Hong Kong among the world's most beautiful urban settings. Vancouver offers twenty-two distinctive neighborhoods including North America's third-largest Chinatown (behind San Francisco and New York), which boasts the first authentic classical Chinese garden ever built outside of China, and spectacular Northwest Coast Indian art.

Vancouver's weather—the mildest in all of Canada thanks to warm Pacific Ocean currents—is an attraction as well. The cliché that one can sail and ski in the same day during a stay in metropolitan Vancouver is entirely true, and one might easily substitute rock climbing, kayaking, SCUBA diving, or board sailing. Vancouver is North America's largest per capita consumer of wine and third only to Los Angeles and New York as a North American film and television production center.

To the west, across the Strait of Georgia, is Vancouver Island, home to Victoria, British Columbia's provincial capital. It was established as a fort by the Hudson's Bay Company and served as a staging area for the great Cariboo Gold Rush in the western Canadian mountains. One should think of Victoria as a respite, a quaint and elegant reminder of more leisured times. It

British Columbia's provincial capital, Victoria, on Vancouver Island, was already a popular tourist destination in 1910. Its two massive stone Parliament buildings, overlooking the Inner Harbour, had been completed thirteen years earlier.

is a small town of just seventy-five-thousand people and is a serene place of tearooms, tartan shops, horse-drawn carriages, and a blitz of flowered window boxes and hanging baskets strung from lampposts. Here, too, the Royal British Columbia Museum chronicles the province's social and natural history. Milepost Zero of the Trans Canada Highway can be found here. So can Fan Tan Alley, the narrowest street in North America, which leads to Canada's oldest Chinatown. Most memorable, perhaps, is the image of British Columbia's 1893 array of Parliament buildings, all outlined in lights that reflect in the waters of Olde Towne's Inner Harbour. After a visit, Rudyard Kipling wrote, "to realize Victoria, you must take all that the eye admires in Bournemouth, Torquay, the Isle of Wight, the happy valley at Hong Kong, the Doon, Sorrento and Camp's Bay—add the reminiscences of the Thousand Islands and arrange the whole around the Bay of Naples with some Himalayas for the background." Only the most fortunate of travelers can appreciate all of these references, but one gets the general idea.

Options on Vancouver Island outside Victoria include beachcombing along the shore of the Saanich Peninsula, catching a whale-watching cruise out of tiny Sidney, cycling forty miles along the Galloping Goose Trail to the site of an abandoned gold mine near Sooke, and following yellow footprints in the pavement leading from the museum in Duncan past forty-one of the town's eighty totem poles. Ferries from Victoria also reach the five tranquil Southern Gulf Islands that advertise "plenty of soft adventure."

Taken as a whole, the Pacific Northwest tests the limits of hyperbole: spectacular, panoramic, sublime. This region, which spans vast forests and shores, deserts and sounds, aeries and plains, great cities and quaint towns, merits these superlatives and at least one more. And, of course, it is incomparably fragrant.

OVERLEAF: Mount Shasta, at 14,162 feet, is the highest peak in the California Cascades and second in height to Washington's Mount Rainier in all the Cascades. It stands apart from other peaks and looms over California's former gold country.

Northern California's Shasta Lake (left), a manmade reservoir created by the damming of the Sacramento and two smaller rivers, is a popular family resort. Visitors can rent houseboats with which they can explore caverns that are difficult to reach by land. Ancient redwood trees (above) line the thirty-three-mile "Avenue of the Giants" in Humboldt Redwoods State Park near the California coast. Millions of these trees—some of which rise three hundred feet or more into the sky— were felled for paper, but national and state parks have since pre- served magnificent specimens. U.S. Route 101 through the area is often called the "Redwood Highway."

If there ever was a classic American Victorian village, it is Ferndale (above), south of Eureka in far-northern California. The blend of agriculture and architecture in the thriving dairy center led to the term "butterfat palaces" to describe the town's many ornately decorated buildings. Ferndale is remarkably well preserved, perhaps in part because of local insistence that buildings conform to the old-town look. "Visit Ferndale," notes the local chamber of commerce in an attractive booklet about the community. "But don't tell too many people." Although the 1906 earthquake that also struck San Francisco destroyed some of Ferndale's shops, most of Main Street's Victorian houses survived. The William Carson Mansion (opposite), built about 1884 in Eureka by a lumber baron, is one of California's most-photographed homes. Now a private club, the building features exotic materials including onyx, white mahogany, and extensive redwood.

Sculptor Dick Crane of Eureka, California, spent three years creating The Fisherman *(above), a solid copper monument to lost mariners on Humboldt Bay's Woodley Island Marina. The figure and his nets and boat weigh more than two thousand pounds. Sometimes nicknamed the "Statue of Liberty of the West Coast," the crusty old salt is the largest known U.S. memorial of its type. Battery Point Light (right) is known to the residents of Crescent City, on California's far-north coast, as the "Christmas Light." First illuminated on Christmas Day 1856, the lighthouse miraculously survived tidal waves that killed ten people and caused $16 million in damage in Crescent City in 1964.*

Natural Bridges Cove (opposite) is a highlight of Boardman State Park on the Oregon Coast. Rock formations that jut from the water near the mouth of Pistol River (top left) look treacherous enough, but the coastline is even more dangerous when deadly waves called tsunamis strike. They are caused by undersea earthquakes that trigger small waves in the open sea that can become high-speed, fifty-foot monsters that batter a shoreline. There are even signs marking tsunami evacuation routes along the Oregon coast. Good-sized islands—and huge offshore kelp beds—pop into view off Port Orford Beach (bottom left). The scene off to sea near Brookings (overleaf) is just as stunning. Oregon boasts more than three hundred miles of sandy, public beaches, easily accessed from U.S. Route 101.

Sunsets (above) are memorable on the Oregon Coast. So are foggy mornings, sunny days, and rainy afternoons. Visitors are often surprised to find the coastline's beaches roomy, towns relatively uncrowded, and vistas uncluttered. Reasons? The ocean temperature is usually nippy, few tourist attractions have been built, and chilly mists often envelop the shore. Average high air temperatures in July range from 62 at Newport to 68 in Astoria. So the Oregon Coast (opposite) attracts campers, horseback riders, nature lovers, fishers, and those who appreciate the staggeringly beautiful juxtaposition of surf, sand, and mountain greenery. Lively wave action attracts sailors, surfers, and windsurfers. More than four hundred gray whales live off the central coast during the summer and they can be seen from a distance on shore or up close on chartered excursions. Another twenty thousand or so are known to pass by in spring and winter.

North of Florence, Oregon, dunes (above) stretch like surf froth forty miles into the distance. Up close (right), many are held together by tufts of sea grass, but others meander with the wind and waves. The Oregon dunes have been preserved as a national recreation area, but limited reserved camping is available. The dunes make a perfect children's playground; dune-buggy riders and mountain bikers cavort under close ranger supervision; and even dogsledders train their teams on the shifting sand. Like California, Oregon has a coastal mountain range (overleaf) as well as higher inland peaks. This view of the Oregon coastal range was taken from Coxcomb Hill high above Astoria.

One of the nation's most-photographed lighthouses is the Haceta Head Light (above) north of Florence on the Oregon Coast. Named for Bruno de Heceta, a Portuguese sailing for the Royal Spanish Navy who first noted the head and surrounding shallow water in 1775 while searching for Sitka, Alaska, the lighthouse has been in continuous service since its wick was first lit in 1894. Its original lamp consumed coal oil at a rate of one-half gallon a day, and a clock mechanism needed to be wound every four hours to ensure the light emitted one white flash per minute. The original keeper's house no longer stands, but the assistant keeper's dwelling can still be seen. Up the coast near Newport, the 162-foot Yaquina Head Lighthouse (opposite), the tallest on the Oregon coast, was first illuminated in 1873. It overlooks a seabird nesting area.

The 4.1-mile-long Astoria Bridge at the mouth of the Columbia River (left) connects Astoria, Oregon, with southwest Washington. Boston fur trader Robert Gray sailed into the river in 1792 and named it after his ship. The Astoria Column (above), on Coxcomb Hill high above town, is a 125-foot cement structure patterned after the Trajan Column in Rome. On it is carved—in a sgraffito pictorial frieze—the region's history. Portland (overleaf), Oregon's largest city, was already a thriving inland port before thousands of newcomers discovered its agreeable climate, innumerable parks and gardens, public artwork, and pedestrian malls. Presciently, Portland enacted a tough "urban growth boundary" to curtail sprawl.

OREGON HISTORY CENTER

WELCOME

1200

Permanent and visiting exhibits at the Oregon History Center (opposite) illuminate the Beaver State's rich history. The building's eight-story trompe l'oeil murals are a landmark in the heart of Portland's Cultural District. The entrance, and marble floor, and wooden benches and ticket counters at the city's Union Station (left) got a facelift in 1996 for the terminal's centennial. Once, 150 trains a day arrived or departed from the station that united three of Henry Villard's passenger rail lines. Today just nine Amtrak trains come or go daily. The station, designed by a Kansas City architectural firm, opened in 1896 on the site of a fifteen-foot-deep lake. The blue and gold neon "GO BY TRAIN" and "UNION STATION" tower signs were added in 1948.

47

Portland boasts more than forty microbreweries and uncounted brewpubs. One of the oldest is the Bridge-Port brewery (left) in the revitalized industrial Pearl District. BridgePort's British-style brews are now distributed in several western states. Some say the city's often misty weather drives its large white-collar workforce inside for coffee and bagels in the morning and at lunch, and into brewpubs in the early evening. Pittock Mansion (above), a twenty-two-room French Renaissance château built by the longtime publisher of Portland's Oregonian newspaper, offers a spectacular view of the city. About half of Oregon's population is concentrated in metropolitan Portland, and more than two-thirds of Oregonians live in a narrow strip along Interstate Highway 5 southward to the California line.

Portland is the "Rose City," with its own International Rose Test Garden (above) and a month-long Rose Festival each June. The festival is marked by a rose parade second in scope only to the famous New Year's Day event in Pasadena, California. The Japanese Gardens (right) in Portland's Washington Park, designed by Takuma Tono in 1963, feature a sand and stone garden, a tea garden, tranquil ponds, and a "flat garden." Portland's temperate, often damp climate at the confluence of the Columbia and Willamette rivers keeps the city green and flowering year-round. City streets are often ablaze in rhododendrons, azaleas, camellias, flowering trees, and colorful beech and other hardwoods.

The Columbia River Gorge (above), looking eastward along America's second-longest river from a viewpoint near Corbett, Oregon, is a magnificent sight as it was to pioneers heading in the opposite direction. In the distance on a high bluff is Vista House, an interpretive center and gift shop. Not until the serpentine Columbia River Scenic Highway below was completed by Samuel Hill in 1915 was vehicular travel possible up or down the river; travel was primarily by raft. Multnomah Falls (opposite), one of Oregon's biggest attractions and one of many waterfalls along the Columbia Gorge, falls 620 feet from a snow-fed creek atop a ridge on Larch Mountain east of Portland. The falls and the surrounding three hundred acres are managed by the U.S. Forest Service. A 1925 stone lodge with two dining rooms offers views of the falls and the Columbia River below.

Furnishings created as a Depression make-work project in Portland melded pioneer and Indian motifs for Timberline Lodge (opposite) midway up the south side of Mount Hood, Oregon's highest mountain. Because beams were hand cut on site from green wood, they cracked extensively as they dried over the years. Works Progress Administration worker Tom Lamon executed this glass mosaic, Bring on the Mountain *(top left), just inside the main lodge door. He used leftover glass from a bigger* Babe the Blue Ox *mural. Indian-theme carvings (bottom left) were copied from Campfire Girl manuals. The Willamette Valley (overleaf) is the state's greenbelt. Flowers harvested for their seeds—the lighter crop—and beans— the darker planting— grow almost within a stone's throw of the state capital in Salem.*

Oregon's Modern Greek–style capitol (above), completed in 1938, replaced a wooden building— one of two capitols destroyed by fire— that was modeled after the U.S. Capitol. Designed by Francis Kelly of the New York firm Trowbridge & Livingston, the new four-story structure is faced in white Danby Vermont marble. The hollow, bronze Oregon Pioneer statue, finished in gold leaf, that tops the building was designed by Ulric Ellerhusen. The heroic figure is reached by 121 steps spiraling up the capitol tower to a deck that provides a spectacular view of Salem. The pioneer theme is continued in massive marble sculptures that flank the main entrance (left). On the back of Leo Friedlander's The Covered Wagon is an intaglio map outlining the old Oregon Trail.

The Aufderheide Memorial Scenic Byway passes peaceful Lookout Point Reservoir (above) in central Oregon. The 1944 Office Bridge (opposite), the state's longest covered bridge, was constructed in the Lane County lumber "company town" of Westfir. Built sturdy with triple trusses and triple beams to carry heavy logging trucks, the bridge connected a mill with the company office. Hence its name. Except for a few tour-boat excursions, Crater Lake (overleaf) is kept free of boats to enhance the visitor experience. The National Park Service maintains more than ninety miles of hiking trails, many that skirt the rim of the ancient lake or ascend promontories. Although the lake was formed by the eruption of Mount Mazama 7,700 years ago, it got its name in 1869 from the small crater at the top of Wizard Island, the cinder cone that rises 760 feet above the lake surface.

Viewpoints at Crater Lake National Park offer vistas of Oregon's Cascade Range (opposite). Ancient shamans forbade most Native Americans from viewing Crater Lake, and it was never mentioned to whites. Finally in 1853, prospectors searching for the Lost Cabin Gold Mine stumbled upon the incredible natural wonder. In 1886, a U.S. Geological Survey calculated the lake's depth at 1,996 feet by dropping piano wire. The figure was very close to the official sonar reading of 1,932 feet recorded in 1959. Rainbow trout and kokanee salmon had to be introduced to the clear, cold lake water by humans, beginning in 1888. Buyer DeWayne Lang and yard manager Doug Goucher—with the sunglasses—are two of thousands of loggers (above) who work in Oregon's huge timber industry. More than forty million board feet are harvested each year in Oregon, Idaho, and Utah by companies based in North Powder, Oregon.

Ranchhand Casey Martin stacks alfalfa hay (above) at the seventeen-hundred-acre V. P. Ranch in North Powder in eastern Oregon. Some of the hay from the irrigated spread is shipped as far as Japan. Casey and his brothers Sam and Drew pose, left to right, with their mounts (right). Four generations of Martins run 200 head of their own cattle and 150 leased animals on their spread. The old Nez Percé Trail runs along the Grande Ronde River Valley (overleaf) in southeast Washington's canyon country. From this homeland in what was then Oregon, Chief Joseph and his Nez Percé followers began a remarkable fifteen-hundred-mile flight from capture in 1877. "My heart is sick and sad," said Joseph upon his surrender in northern Montana.

Even after a visit to Oregon and its awe-inspiring mountains, forests, and craggy coastline, one can easily forget that almost two thirds of the state—and of Washington to the north as well—is relatively flat and agricultural. Wheat (left) is a thriving Oregon crop. An 1879 one-room schoolhouse (above) was moved from Pilot Rock, Oregon, to downtown Pendleton in 1990 and placed next to the old Union Pacific Depot. The latter now houses the Umatilla County Historical Society Museum. In the 1840s and 1850s, Pendleton was almost the end of the Oregon Trail. But first the dauntless settlers on that Great Migration faced one last, treacherous trek through the Blue Mountains—before the first snow—to the lush promised land of the Willamette Valley to the west.

Explorers Meriwether Lewis and William Clark took note of Hat Rock (opposite) near Umatilla, Oregon, along the Columbia River. Across the River in a county park at Wallula Gap in Washington, the Two Sisters formation (above)—like Hat Rock—was formed when its sturdier basalt columns withstood the erosion that swept away surrounding sandstone. According to Native American legend, a spiritual hero named Coyote turned his two wives into these two pillars of rock. America's own Stonehenge (overleaf), near Goldendale in south-central Washington, was the nation's first monument to the dead of World War I. The replica of the mysterious structure on Salisbury Plain in Wilshire, England, was built by wealthy entrepreneur—and pacifist—Sam Hill as a monument to thirteen Klickitat County men who were "sacrificed to the god of war." Hill's nearby mansion is now the Maryhill Museum of Art.

Apple crates (above) are stacked and ready for pickers near Richland, Washington. Richland and its sister Tri-Cities, Pasco and Kennewick, are bustling agricultural centers. Hops grow up networks of twine near Grandview, Washington (opposite), where summertime temperatures often exceed one hundred degrees Fahrenheit—ideal for growing this bitter vine. The ready accessibility of this savory ingredient, and to sparkling mountain stream water, helps account for the surfeit of breweries of all sizes throughout the Pacific Northwest. Yakima Valley (overleaf) is world-renowned for its apples and of late has emerged as a prosperous wine region. Rafters flock to the valley each fall for the annual "Flip Flop," when a torrent of water is released from Rimrock Lake down the Tieton River and into the Naches River to facilitate irrigation. This more than doubles the Tieton's normal flow to 2,500 cubic feet per second.

The classic 1891 Review *building (opposite) is a Spokane landmark. It housed the offices of the* Review, *and later those of the city's combined dailies. (See a historic view within the Spokane skyline on page 16.) One of three falls of the Spokane River (above) helps power the city's electric plant. The falls, where early residents of "Spokane Falls" scooped up spawning salmon, are among many sites enjoyed by strollers in Riverfront Park in the city's core. Others in this relaxing downtown green belt include a hand-carved 1909 carousel, a science center, and a gondola whose course spans the churning white water. Nearby are the city's convention center, an international "ag trade center," and an elegant opera house—all legacies of the city's Expo '74. Indeed, the entire one-hundred-acre Riverfront Park was created for this vibrant city's ambitious world's fair.*

In 1898, prominent Spokane architect Kirtland Kelsey Cutter built a lavish Tudor Revival–style mansion (top right) for mine owner Amasa B. Campbell who made a fortune in the Coeur d'Alene mining district of northern Idaho. The house is now part of the local historical society's museum complex. Also in 1898, Cutter built another elegant home nearby (bottom right) for Patrick "Patsy" Clark, another millionaire miner. Clark instructed Cutter to spare no expense in creating the most elegant home in the West, so Cutter traveled the world in search of materials and fixtures. Inside the house, which is now a popular restaurant, each room follows a different architectural style. Spokane's Riverfront Clock Tower (opposite) was built above the city train station by the Great Northern Railroad in 1902.

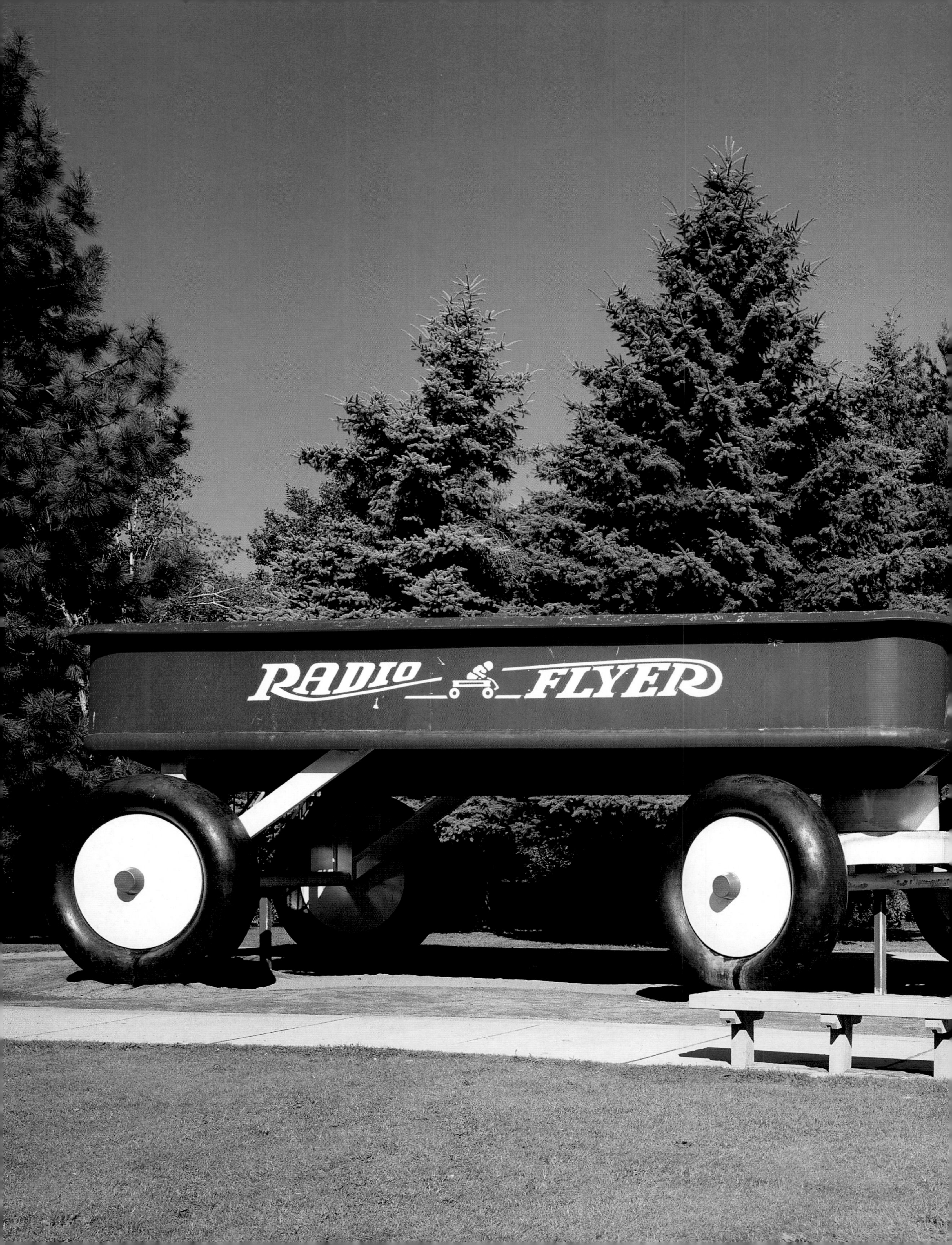
RADIO FLYER

Ken Spiering's Child-
hood Express *red
wagon sculpture (left)
in Spokane's River-
front Park, created to
honor Washington
State's centennial in
1989, offers a fun slide
and a fine river view.
Several businesses
and civic organiza-
tions donated the
piece to the children
of Spokane. Sculpture
takes a western twist
(above) in a park
in little Ritzville in*
*southeast Washing-
ton. Two decades
after the eruption of
the Mount Saint
Helens volcano in
southwest Washington
(see page 12), the
effects of the devasta-
tion—created in a
few minutes of cata-
clysmic explosions
and fire—can still
be plainly seen (over-
leaf). The area is now
a "volcanic monu-
ment" overseen by the
U.S. Forest Service.*

Stampede Pass (above), on the main east-west highway across Washington to Seattle, is home to abundant wildlife including elk, black bears, and bobcats. Deeper in the north-woods, some terrified visitors swear they've encountered another life form: Sasquatch, or "Bigfoot," a gangly, hairy, shy, and (said to be) smelly hominoid. Until one of these creatures is captured, scientists remain *skeptical of the sight-ings and purported Sasquatch footprints. On a clear day, the icebound summit of Mount Rainier (right) is clearly visible from down-town Seattle or Tacoma. British explorer George Vancouver named the peak for his friend and fellow admiral, Peter Rainier. Riffe Lake (overleaf), south of Tacoma, graces the Toutle Mountain Range.*

Bob "Sully" Sullivan displays his peppers and other produce at the Olympia farmers' market (above), the state's second-largest behind Pike Place in Seattle. Sullivan brings more than fifty varieties of peppers to the market, which is open Thursdays through Sundays from April until Christmas in the state capital. A statue to the heroes of "the World War"— World War I—frames the Washington State Capitol in Olympia (opposite). The inscription reads: "Their sacrifice was to vindicate the principles of peace and justice in the world." The capitol is actually several buildings; the 287-foot dome of the neo-Roman–style Legislative Building, completed in 1927, was inspired by the U.S. Capitol in Washington, D.C. The capitol complex's gardens, conservatory, rows of Japanese cherry trees, modern state library, and nearby State Capitol Museum all draw visitors, especially in summertime.

Tacoma's old Union Station (opposite) is now a United States courthouse. Larry Anderson's New Beginnings *statue* celebrated Tacoma's centennial in 1984. Before it repackaged its image around jet aircraft and its Space Needle, Seattle was known as the City of Clocks (left and above). Early in the twentieth century, fifty-five or more street, or post, clocks adorned downtown streets. They were ticking testimonials, especially for jewelry stores that maintained most of them. Many were painted dark "street clock green"; others were red, in the faint hope that truckers and other drivers might see and avoid them. In 1953, Seattle's board of public works banned street clocks except those that owners guaranteed to keep running and accurate. By the 1990s, only nine working clocks remained.

Rooms are no longer seventy-five cents at the State Hotel (above), just off Pioneer Square in Seattle. In fact there are no rooms to be had. A New Orleans–style restaurant took over the ground floor, and the building's owner, architect Karl Weiss—who helped save Pike Place Market from the clutches of developers—lives upstairs. Pioneer Square, too, was saved from decay. During the period following the Klondike Gold Rush, the area became a woebegone Skid Row festooned with flophouses, brothels, and rough saloons. The popular Underground Seattle Tour takes visitors . . . underground! (opposite) to the street level that existed more than a century ago. It is dark, dank, endlessly fascinating— and out of the rain— down there. A similar musty experience awaits visitors to Pendleton in northeast Oregon, too. Tunnels beneath that city lead to old bordellos and Chinese living quarters.

Pioneer Square (opposite) was Seattle's first neighborhood. The ornate pergola, or girdered arbor, was erected in 1905 to shelter patrons of a vast underground lavatory and patrons waiting for the cable car. James Wehr's sculpture of Chief Seattle (left) atop a fountain on the square was commissioned by park commissioners in 1909. One of the nation's smallest national historical sites is the Klondike Gold Rush National Historical Park in Seattle (overleaf). It is a companion to a more expansive park in Skagway, Alaska. The Klondike Gold Rush was triggered in Seattle in 1897 when miners unloaded more than two tons of gold. Thousands of "sourdough" prospectors, and many disappointed dreamers, bought provisions in town and set off for Skagway, which was the gateway to the Canadian Yukon gold fields.

Jonathan Borofsky's Hammering Man statue (above) "hammers" silently four times per minute outside the Seattle Art Museum. The twenty-six thousand–pound fabricated steel statue stands forty-eight feet tall. Seattle's waterfront-route streetcar (right) stops at Occidental Park off Pioneer Square. The park features several totem poles, not including one that drunken city fathers stole from a Tlingit Indian village up the coast in 1890. When an arsonist burned that pole in 1938, the city sent a $5,000 check to the Tlingits to carve a replacement. Legend has it that the burghers received this note in return: "Thanks for finally paying for the first one. A new pole will cost another $5,000."

Seattle's Pike Place Market (left) rivals New Orleans's French Market as an abundant in-city farmers' market. With its profusion of vegetables, flowers, fish, baked goods, and handicrafts, the market draws as many tourists as locals. Coffee insignias are signs of the times (above). One would think Seattle would be perpetually "wired" on caffeine judging from the number of chains—including Starbucks and Seattle's Best Coffee—that started there, and many a streetcorner offers other java houses as well. Seattlites say their coffee addiction stems more from the sophistication of the high-tech workforce than from the sometimes-dreary climate that cries out for a "jump start" to the day.

The Pike Place Fish Company draws a crowd not just for its selection of Alaskan king crabs, halibut, or Coho or sockeye salmon, but also for the show put on by "fish throwers" like "The Bear" (above). When a customer selects a fish, Bear and other throwers toss the clammy creature over the counter to the barking encouragement of the waiting fishwrappers. These entertaining fishmon-gers even have their own website: www. fishthrowers.com. Down the row in Seattle's public market is Manzo Bros. fruit stand (right), where Karen Harrington presides over local and Yakima Valley pro-duce. Begun in 1907 as an open-air gathering spot for farm wagons, Pike Place Market almost succumbed to later urban renewal, but it was declared a historical site, saved, and refurbished.

One of the best "photo ops" in all of the Pacific Northwest can be found across the Tacoma Narrows Bridge in pleasant Gig Harbor (opposite). Distant Mount Rainier is framed against the bobbing masts of hundreds of tiny sailboats. The bridge to Gig Harbor is worth a note, too, because it replaced the notorious "Galloping Gerdie," a perpetually shifting and unstable bridge that finally collapsed in 1940. Fat Smitty's Diner (top left) is a roadside attraction in Discovery Bay on the Olympic Peninsula. Opened in 1942, it features burgers, fries, and a strict two-beer limit. Espresso stands are ubiquitous throughout the Pacific Northwest, even in small towns like Port Angeles on the peninsula where the drive-through Latté Express (bottom left) serves both plain and flavored espresso drinks.

Washington's Olympic Peninsula, the thumb that sticks upward toward Alaska to the west of Puget Sound, is the northwestern tip of the continental United States. It is a world apart—rainier and foggier than the rest of the state, and surprisingly mountainous. Ferns and forest flowers like foxglove and lupine abound in Olympic National Forest (above). There is even a designated rain forest (opposite) with even lusher vegetation. The peninsula's soaring Olympic Mountains trap clouds moving inland off the Pacific Ocean in a "rain shadow." The result is that areas to the west are among the wettest in the entire Pacific Northwest while areas to the east are the driest. Lake Crescent (overleaf) takes its name from its crescent shape. In 1937, President Roosevelt met there with federal and state officials, leading to creation of the far-ranging national forest. The lake's original lodges, built in 1915, are still in use.

The Sequim-
Dungeness Valley
Chamber of Com-
merce on the Olympic
Peninsula displays
a fetching model of
the nearby New Dun-
geness Lighthouse
(above). Near Sequim
a large and now
famous herd of elk is
fond of crossing
Highway 101 under
the watchful eye of fish
and game officials and
sightseers. A Washing-
ton State Ferry boat
from Anacortes docks
at Friday Harbor

(right) in the San
Juan Islands. Ferries
stop at the four largest
of 176 named islands
in the San Juan
Archipelago in Puget
Sound. The islands
draw hikers, bicyclists,
whale watchers,
and others looking
to escape the urban
rat race. Anacortes
itself is on an island,
Fidalgo, just offshore
from the Washington
mainland (overleaf).
Ferry passengers at
dusk can often enjoy
a spectacular sunset.

The Peace Arch (opposite) at the crossing into Canada near Blaine, Washington, was the idea of world traveler Sam Hill, about whom the expression, "Where in the Sam Hill is he?" originated. Hill, president of the Pacific Highway Association, wanted to salute the world's longest undefended border. The arch, built in 1920, is jointly managed by Washington and British Columbia. Washington schoolchildren paid for the separate Peace Gardens nearby (above); down the green is another flower bed laid out to resemble Canada's national flag. Vancouver's spectacular skyline (overleaf) conceals innumerable parks. The city, whose motto is "Spectacular by Nature," was the setting for the popular TV series The X Files, and its varied terrain has served as a movie double for Seattle in Stakeout, for New York in Look Who's Talking, Detroit in Bird on a Wire, and even Beverly Hills in Harry Crumb.

The world's first known steam-powered clock (opposite) is a big draw in Vancouver. Built by horologist Raymond Saunders in 1977, the two-ton, cast-bronze Gastown Steam Clock whistles Westminster chimes each quarter-hour and spews forth steam each hour. Its "falling ball" movement is powered by steam fed from underground pipes. Totem poles (top left) are one attraction at Vancouver's Stanley Park, which a local writer described as a "thousand-acre therapeutic couch." Canada's largest urban greensward was originally a military reserve guarding Vancouver harbor from aggressive Americans. The park is named for Sir Frederick Arthur Stanley, governor general of Canada, after whom hockey's Stanley Cup trophy is also named. Canada Place (bottom left), Vancouver's world trade center, features retail shops, a ferry terminal, and a food court.

One of the most dazzling sights in all of the Pacific Northwest is the British Columbia Parliament Building complex that overlooks Victoria's Inner Harbour and is outlined by more than three thousand lights at night (left). It is a tradition that goes as far back as anyone in town can remember. Atop the central dome is a statue of Captain George Vancouver, the first European to circumnavigate what became Vancouver Island. Out front is a statue, requisite for the times on British government buildings, of dour Queen Victoria, for whom the city is named. Victoria is a city of boutiques, antique shops, pubs, and small hotels. And it is also a city of flowers, notably hanging baskets of blooms (above) that adorn railings and balconies all over town.

Some of the world's most magnificent floral plantings can be found at Butchart Gardens, a fifty-acre 1904 country estate on the Saanich Peninsula near Victoria. Among many dazzling stops are the Japanese Garden (above) and the Italian Gardens (right). In the summertime, this far north in the hemisphere, daylight lasts late into the evening and bathes the blossoms, flowering trees and shrubs, greenhouses, and lagoons. More than seven hundred varieties of flowers, some exotic, can be found at Butchart Gardens. Victoria's love for flowers began when British soldiers planted roses in what was then a Pacific wilderness to remind them of home. Each February, Victorians even count their blossoms, sometimes with calculators in hand, and report totals to a central location. It is their ritual farewell to winter.

Index

Page numbers in italics refer to illustrations.

Aberdeen, Washington, 19
Anacortes, Washington, *18, 114*
Anderson, Larry, 95
Astor, John Jacob, 10

Near Victoria stands Fisgard Lighthouse, a sentinel at Fort Rodd Hill Canadian National Historic Park. The first permanent lighthouse on Vancouver Island's western shore, Fisgard was illuminated by the British in 1860 and was automated in 1928. The fort's gun emplacements guarded Victoria and a big naval base at Esquimalt from 1878 to 1956. Some of its batteries and bunkers still stand.

Astoria, Oregon and the Astoria Column, 8, 13, *35, 36, 43*
Astoria Bridge, *53*
Aufderheide Memorial Scenic Byway, *60*
Avenue of the Giants, 12, *25*

Battery Point Light, *28*
Bear Flag Republic, 12
Beer and breweries, 8–9, 14, *49*
Bierstadt, Albert, *7*
Bigfoot, 88
Blue Mountains, 10
Booth, Michael, *4*
Borofsky, Jonathan, *17, 102*
BridgePort Brewery, Portland, 8, *49*
Bring on the Mountain mosaic, *55*
British settlement and boundary disputes, 11
Brookings, Oregon, *31*
Butchart Gardens, *7, 126*

Campbell House mansion, Spokane, 16, *82*
Carson Mansion, Eureka, *26*
Cascade Range and Cascade Loop, 9, *18, 21,* 65

Chief Joseph, *66*
Chief Seattle sculpture, *99*
Childhood Express red wagon sculpture, *85*
Clark, "Patsy" (restaurant), Spokane, 16, *82*
Coffee craze, 7–8, *105, 109*
Columbia River, gorge, and highway, 8, 9, 10, 11, *11,* 13, 14, *43, 50, 52, 73*
Corbett, Oregon, *52*
Covered bridge, *60*
Crane, Dick, 28
Crater Lake, *4,* 12, 14, *60, 65*
Crescent City, California, *28*
Cutter, Kirtland Kelsey, *82*

Dunes, Oregon, *36*

Eastern Oregon, 15, *66, 71*
Eastern Washington, 13, 14, 15–16, *66, 85*
Eureka, California, 12, *26, 28*

Fat Smitty's Diner, Discovery Bay, *109*
Ferndale Victorian village, 13, *26*
Fish throwers, *106*
Fisgard Lighthouse, *128*
Fisherman, The (statue), *28*
Fort Rodd Hill, *128*
Friday Harbor, *114*

Gig Harbor, Washington, *109*
Grande Ronde River Valley, *66*
Grandview, Washington, *76*
Gray, Robert, 10, *43*

Haceta Head Light, *40*
Hammering Man statue, *17, 102*
Hanford nuclear plant, 17
Hat Rock formation, *73*
Hill, Sam, *73, 119*

John Day, Oregon, 15

Klondike Gold Rush and museum, *18, 96, 99*

Lady Washington tall ship, *19*
La Grande, Oregon, 15
Lake Crescent, *110*
Latte Express, Port Angeles, *109*
Lewis and Clark expedition and trail, 10, 13
Lighthouses, *28, 40, 114, 128*
Lookout Point Reservoir, *60*

Manzo Bros. fruit stand, *106*

Martin Family Ranch, North Powder, Oregon, *66*
McCall, Tom, 14
Mount Baker, *9*
Mount Hood, *7,* 9, *10,* 12, 14, *55*
Mount Lassen, 12
Mount Ranier, *9,* 12, *21, 88, 109*
Mount Saint Helens, 12, *12, 85*
Mount Shasta, *9,* 12, *21*
Multnomah Falls, 14, *52*

Native Americans, *4,* 8, *8,* 65, *99, 102*
Natural Bridges Cove, *31*
New Beginnings statue, *95*
New Dungeness Lighthouse, *114*
Nez Percé Trail, *66*

Occidental Park, *102*
Office Bridge, *60*
Olympia, Washington, 20, *92*
Olympic Peninsula, mountains, and rain forest, *7,* 19, *109, 110, 114*
Oregon Coast, 13, *31, 35, 36,* 40
Oregon History Center, *47*
Oregon Pioneer statue, *59*
Oregon State Capitol, *59*
Oregon Territory, 11
Oregon Trail, *4,* 10, 15, *59, 71*

Parliament Building complex, Victoria, *21, 125*
Peace Garden and arch, 20, *119*
Pendleton, Oregon, *4,* 15, *71, 96*
Pike Place Market, Seattle, 17, *96, 105, 106*
Pioneer Square, Seattle, 17, 20, *96, 99, 102*
Pittock Mansion, *49*
Portland, 7, 10, 14, *43, 47, 49, 50*
Port Orford Beach, Oregon, *31*

Redwood Forest and highway, 12, *25*
Review Building, Spokane, 16, *81*
Richland, Washington, 15, *17, 76*
Riffe Lake, 88
Ritzville, Washington, *85*
Riverfront Park and tower, Spokane, 16, *81, 82*
Rose Test Garden, Portland, *50*
Roseburg, Oregon and "Graffiti Weekend," 14–15

Russian settlement, 10

Sacramento River and valley, 12, *25*
Salem, Oregon, *55, 59*
San Juan Islands, *9, 18, 114*
Seattle, *4, 7,* 17–18, *18, 19, 20,* 88, *95, 96, 99, 102, 105, 106*
Shasta Lake, 12, *25*
Shasta, Mount, *see* Mount Shasta
Snake River, *9*
Space Needle, *4,* 17, *95*
Spiering, Ken, *85*
Spokane, 16, *16, 81, 82, 85*
Stampede Pass, 88
Stanley Park, Vancouver, *4, 123*
State Hotel, Seattle, *96*
Stonehenge monument, *73*
Steam clock, Gastown, Vancouver, *123*
Street clocks, Seattle, 19, *95*

Tacoma, 19–20, *88, 95*
Tacoma Narrows Bridge, *109*
Tillamook and Tillamook Creamery, *9,* 13
Timber industry, 65
Timberline Lodge, 14, *55*
Totems, *4,* 20, *102, 123*
Tri-Cities of Washington, 15–16, *76*
Tsunamis, *31*
Two Sisters formation, *73*

Underground Seattle, 20, *96*
Union Station, Portland, *47*
Union Station, Tacoma, *95*

Vancouver, *4,* 20, *119, 123*
Victoria and Vancouver Island, 11, *18,* 20–21, *21, 125, 126, 128*
Vista House, *52*
V. P. Ranch, Oregon, *66*

Wagons Ho! statue, Pendleton, *4*
Walla Walla, Washington, 15–16
Washington Park, Portland, *50*
Washington State Capitol, Olympia, *92*
Wehr, James, *99*
Weiss, Karl, *96*
Willamette Valley, 10, *55, 71*

Yakima Valley, 16, *17, 76, 106*
Yaquina Head Lighthouse, *40*

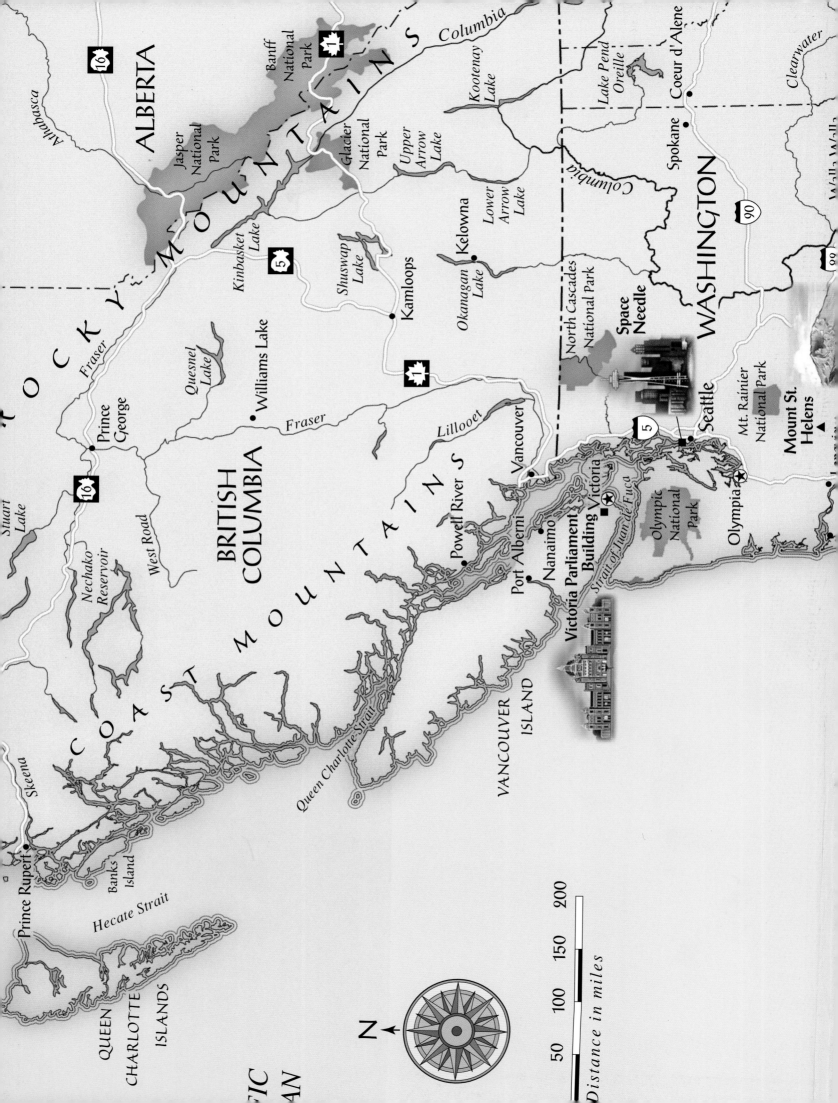

Columbia

ALBERTA

16

Athabasca

Jasper
National
Park

Banff
National
Park

1

R O C K Y   M O U N T A I N S

Kootenay
Lake

Upper
Arrow
Lake

Kinbasket
Lake

5

Shuswap
Lake

Kamloops

Okanagan
Lake

Lower
Arrow
Lake

Kelowna

Columbia

Lake Pend
Oreille

Coeur d'Alene

Spokane

Clearwater

90

WASHINGTON

99

Fraser

Quesnel
Lake

Prince
George

Williams Lake

Fraser

Lillooet

1

North Cascades
National Park

**Space
Needle**

16

**BRITISH
COLUMBIA**

Stuart
Lake

Nechako
Reservoir

West Road

Powell River

Vancouver

5

Seattle

Mt. Rainier
National Park

**Mount St.
Helens**

C O A S T   M O U N T A I N S

Skeena

Port Alberni

Nanaimo

Victoria Parliament
Building

Victoria

Strait of Juan de Fuca

Olympic
National
Park

Olympia

Prince Rupert

Banks
Island

**VANCOUVER
ISLAND**

Queen Charlotte Strait

**QUEEN
CHARLOTTE
ISLANDS**

Hecate Strait

**PACIFIC
OCEAN**

50   100   150   200

Distance in miles

N